MEATS

Junior League of Worcester & 83 Other American Community Recipes

THE KITCHEN

C•O•L•L•E•C•T•I•O•N

Published by THE WIMMER COMPANIES, INC., Memphis, TN in corporate partnership with SHADCA, Inc., Shreveport, LA under the imprint, The Kitchen Collection.

The Wimmer Companies
Memphis, Tennessee

THE KITCHEN
C•O•L•L•E•C•T•I•O•N

ISBN: 1-882232-04-6

For additional copies, please use the order form in back of book or call
The Wimmer Companies, Inc.
1-800-727-1034

INTRODUCTION

THE KITCHEN COLLECTION introduces a series that has been hand-picked from the files of over one million private recipes. They were originally assembled for Community Cookbooks, a book form that is quietly Preserving American Regional Traditions™ by publishing the finest recipes from communities coast to coast.

The recipes have been carefully selected by food-type and put in an easy-to-use format. We wish you good eating as you gather 'round your table to enjoy the foods presented here from the rich heritage of our nation's volunteers.

A portion of your purchase price will support such programs as those that prevent child abuse, fight homelessness and protect the environment.

BARBEQUE BRISKET

5 to 6 pound brisket of beef
Celery salt
Onion and garlic salt
2 ounces liquid smoke
Worcestershire sauce
Prepared barbeque sauce

Sprinkle brisket generously with celery salt, onion salt, garlic salt, liquid smoke, and Worcestershire sauce. Cover with heavy duty aluminum foil and refrigerate overnight. Remove meat from refrigerator and place in a large roasting pan, fat side up. Cover tightly with foil and bake at 275° for about 5 hours. Uncover. Pour ¾ cup barbeque sauce over brisket. Bake for another hour. Remove from oven. Pour off sauce and refrigerate. Refrigerate meat. This allows cold brisket to be thinly sliced. To serve, reheat sauce, adding more barbeque sauce to taste. 12 Servings.

CordonBluegrass
Junior League of Louisville, Inc., Louisville, Kentucky

BARBECUED STEAK

2 pounds flank or round steak, ½-inch thick
1 teaspoon oregano leaves
1½ teaspoons garlic salt
2 tablespoons vegetable oil
2 tablespoons vinegar
1 (8-ounce) can tomato sauce

Score surface of meat ⅛-inch deep in diamond design. Place steak in shallow pan. Mix oregano leaves, garlic salt and oil; spread on steak. Drizzle vinegar over steak. Cover pan with aluminum foil; refrigerate 1 hour or longer. Open can of tomato sauce and place at edge of grill to warm. Place steak on grill 4 inches from hot coals. Grill about 5 minutes on each side, basting frequently with tomato sauce. To serve, cut steak diagonally across the grain into thin slices. Slicing the steak at an angle and the tenderizing effect of the marinade are what make this steak especially appealing. 6 Servings.

Seasoned With Sun
Junior League of El Paso, Inc. El Paso, Texas

BARBECUE

Boil fresh pork or ham. Let simmer 6 to 7 hours with the following:

28 ounces canned tomatoes
5 ounces soy sauce
4 or 5 large onions, chopped
4 or 5 garlic buds, chopped
½ cup brown sugar
½ cup cider vinegar
Worcestershire sauce and hot pepper sauce, to taste
Salt and pepper, to taste

Cool; remove fat and skim off fat juice. Cut meat into small pieces or mash with fork. Use leftover sauce for meat. 6 to 8 Servings.

Savannah Style
Junior League of Savannah, Inc., Savannah, Georgia

BEST EVER BRISKET

Beef brisket, about 10 to 11 pounds
Salt and pepper
2 large onions, sliced
¼ to ½ cup flour
1 cup water

Place meat fat side up in a large deep pan. Add water to ½-inch depth in pan bottom. Salt and pepper meat freely. Arrange onion slices on top; cover with foil and bake at 300° for 8 to 9 hours. When done, remove brisket to warm platter. Skim off fat from pan drippings and add a mixture of flour and water. Boil, stirring constantly for 3 to 5 minutes. Remove from heat and serve on top of meat.

Lone Star Legacy
Austin Junior Forum, Inc., Austin, Texas

Chili Cheese Steaks

2 pounds round steak, cut 1-inch thick
3 tablespoons flour
2 teaspoons salt
2 teaspoons chili powder
¼ teaspoon pepper
¼ cup shortening
2 cups chopped onion
1 (16-ounce) can whole tomatoes
1 (4-ounce) package Cheddar cheese

Preheat oven to 350°. In a large skillet, brown meat in shortening and place in a 9 x 13-inch baking dish. Brown onions until tender and stir in remaining ingredients except cheese. Add to meat. Bake 2 hours. Add grated cheese on top and bake 5 minutes longer. 4 to 6 Servings.

Celebrate San Antonio
San Antonio Junior Forum, San Antonio, Texas

EYE OF ROUND

1 (4- to 5-pound) eye of round
Seasoned salt flavor enhancer
Salt and pepper to taste
Meat tenderizer
Garlic powder
Worcestershire sauce

Stab roast well all over. Sprinkle with meat tenderizer, flavor enhancer, garlic powder, salt, and pepper. Rub in Worcestershire sauce. Stab again all over and sprinkle with more tenderizer, flavor enhancer, and garlic powder. Bake at 225° for 2 to 3 hours for rare. 10 Servings.

Southern Elegance
Junior League of Gaston County, North Carolina

FILLETS MIGNON, SHALLOT SAUCE

4 tablespoons butter
4 fillets of beef, 1-inch thick
Salt and pepper
2 tablespoons shallots, chopped
½ cup dry white wine
Parsley

Melt 3 tablespoons butter in a skillet; brown meat for 4 minutes on each side over high heat. Season with salt and pepper. Place on hot platter and keep warm. To the pan juices in skillet add shallots, wine and remaining tablespoon of butter. Mix well and cook over medium heat for 2 minutes. Spoon over fillets. Garnish with chopped parsley. 4 Servings.

The Mount Vernon Cookbook
The Mount Vernon Ladies' Association of the Union, Mount Vernon, Virginia

GARY'S PORTERHOUSE STEAK

1 (2- to 3-pound) Porterhouse steak (about 2- inches thick)
Salt and pepper
¼ cup soy sauce
½ teaspoon wine vinegar
¾ cup chopped onion
2 cloves garlic, minced
Celery salt
½ teaspoon ground ginger

Cut pocket in each side of steak; fill with combination of onion, garlic, dash of salt, pepper and celery salt. Marinate 1 to 2 hours in soy sauce, wine vinegar and ground ginger. Cook over hot coals 25 minutes, or done to your taste. Turn often and brush with marinade occasionally.

Talk About Good
Junior League of Lafayette, Inc., Lafayette, Louisiana

GINNY'S ROAST

1 (2- to 3-pound) pork roast
1 (8-ounce) jar mustard
1 large onion, thinly sliced
1 tablespoon vinegar

Preheat oven to 275°. Place roast in large dish. Cover top and sides of roast with mustard. Next cover with sliced onions. Add one inch of water to bottom pan; add vinegar. Bake at least six hours at 275°. Roast will become black, crusty and delicious. 6 Servings.

Georgia On My Menu
Junior League of Cobb-Marietta, Inc., Marietta, Georgia

MEAT LOAF

1¼ pounds ground beef
¾ pound ground pork
1½ cups Progresso bread crumbs
1 package Lipton onion soup mix
⅔ cup warm water
⅓ cup catsup
2 eggs, beaten

Combine all ingredients and put in 9x5-inch loaf pan. Bake uncovered at 350° for 1 to 1½ hours. 8 Servings.

Cane River Cuisine
Service League of Natchitoches, Inc., Natchitoches, Louisiana

GREEN PEPPER STEAK

1 pound round steak, cut into strips
¼ cup salad oil
1 clove garlic
1 tablespoon soy sauce
1 onion, chopped
½ cup chopped celery
2 green peppers, chopped
Cornstarch
1 (4-ounce) can mushrooms

Marinate meat in mixture of oil, garlic and soy sauce for several hours or overnight. Brown meat with marinade. Add onion, celery and green peppers. Cook over high heat for several minutes. Reduce heat. Thicken mixture with small amount of cornstarch mixed with water. Add mushroom with liquid and simmer until tender. Add additional soy sauce if desired. Serve over rice or noodles. 8 Servings.

Cane River Cuisine
Service League of Natchitoches, Inc., Natchitoches, Louisiana

GRILLED ROAST BEEF

Almost anything tastes better cooked outside. This roast is no exception, and it is SO much more fun to cook.

3 to 5 pound sirloin tip roast or boneless rump roast
Italian dressing (bottled)
Lemon-pepper marinade

Place roast in glass or plastic container. Pour in Italian dressing, about ½-inch deep. Sprinkle with lemon-pepper marinade. cover and refrigerate for 24 hours, turning once. Grill over coals, as you would a steak. Time depends on how well done you like your meat. I have found that a 3- to 3½-pound roast takes about 1 to 1½ hours. Be sure to sprinkle with lemon-pepper before grilling.

Cotton Country Cooking
Decatur Junior Service League, Inc., Decatur, Alabama

HERB MARINATED TENDERLOIN

1 cup soy sauce
½ cup olive oil
1 cup port wine
1 teaspoon thyme
1 bay leaf
4 cloves garlic
1 teaspoon salt
1 teaspoon coarsely ground black pepper
½ teaspoon hot sauce
1 (5- to 6-pound) tenderloin

Mix all of the ingredients. Marinate the meat for at least 24 hours. Bake in marinade at 425° for 45 minutes for rare. For medium well, bake at 425° for 45 minutes and reduce heat to 325° for 45 minutes. 8 to 10 Servings.

Land of Cotton
John T. Morgan Academy, Selma, Alabama

HOBO STEAK

2½ pounds sirloin steak, 2½-inches thick
1 teaspoon seasoned salt
2 tablespoons garlic spread
1 teaspoon seasoned pepper
2 tablespoons salad oil
1 cup Italian bread crumbs

Remove fat from steak. Make paste of seasonings and spread over meat. Cover with crumbs. Place in brown paper bag and secure tightly. Place on cookie sheet and bake at 375° for 30 minutes, then at 425° for 15 minutes. Remove any paste on bag and spread on sliced meat. 4 to 6 Servings.

RSVP
Junior League of Portland, Maine, Inc.

LAZY MAN'S ROAST

1 (3½- to 8-pound) eye of round roast beef or tenderloin

Salt, pepper and lemon-pepper seasoning, to taste

Preheat oven to highest possible setting. Sprinkle roast with salt pepper, and lemon-pepper. Place on rack in shallow roasting. Bake only **four minutes per pound**. Turn off oven; **do not open door**. Leave roast in oven for 1½ to 2 hours. If desired warm, reheat in moderate oven, but be careful not to overcook. (The roast will be pink on the inside.) 8 to 10 Servings.

Perennials

Junior Service League of Gainesville, Georgia, Inc.

MANHANDLER STEAK WITH GRAVY

Salt and pepper, to taste
¾ pound round steak, tenderized
Small amount of oil
½ envelope of onion soup mix
1 can cream of mushroom soup, slightly diluted with water
¾ cup water

Salt and pepper steak. Lightly brown in small amount of oil. Remove steak and place it in a casserole dish. Sprinkle onion soup mix over steak. Pour mushroom soup and water over all. Cover and bake at 325° until steak is tender, for 2 hours. Check often and add water when needed. 4 Servings.

The Wild Wild West
The Junior League of Odessa, Inc., Odessa, Texas

MARINATED FLANK STEAK

Flank steak (2-pounds or less)
¼ cup soy sauce
3 tablespoons honey
2 tablespoons cider vinegar
1½ teaspoons garlic salt
1½ teaspoons ground ginger
¾ cup oil
1 small onion, chopped fine

Prepare the meat by scoring about ¼-inch deep on each side and removing any fat or membrane. Combine the other ingredients and pour over the meat. Marinate meat overnight in refrigerator or on kitchen counter for at least 4 hours. Remove meat from marinade and grill over charcoal for 10 minutes on each side. Slice thinly on the diagonal. 3 to 4 Servings.

Savannah Style
Junior League of Savannah, Inc., Savannah, Georgia

MARINATED LONDON BROIL

¼ cup soy sauce
2 tablespoons vinegar
3 tablespoons honey
1½ teaspoons garlic chips
1½ teaspoons ground ginger
¾ cup vegetable oil
1½- to 2-pound London broil

Mix all ingredients and pour over meat. Refrigerate at least overnight. Grill over very hot coals 5 minutes on each side. It is best served rare. This meat is wonderful chilled after grilling and then sliced and served for picnics. 6 Servings.

Georgia On My Menu
Junior League of Cobb-Marietta, Inc., Marietta, Georgia

MARINATED ROAST OR STEAK

4 pounds round roast or round steak
1 bottle separating French dressing
½ cup red cooking wine with garlic or white cooking wine
1 package meat marinade
2 tablespoons Worcestershire sauce

Mix together and marinate for 24 hours, turning and basting occasionally. Cook on grill, with cover, using indirect cooking until it is as done as desired.

Cotton Country Cooking
Decatur Junior Service League, Inc., Decatur, Alabama

MARINATED TENDERLOIN

Must prepare ahead.

1 cup soy sauce
4 garlic cloves, finely chopped
1 beef tenderloin, whole and trimmed
⅓ cup olive oil
½ cup sherry

Mix soy sauce, garlic, olive oil, and sherry together and marinate tenderloin for several hours or overnight turning several times. When ready to cook, roast on rack in 425° oven for 28 to 30 minutes. Baste with marinade from time to time. 8 to 10 Servings.

Southern Elegance
Junior League of Gaston County, North Carolina

ROAST BEEF FLAUTAS

12 corn tortillas
1 cup roast beef, shaved (great for leftovers)
1 cup shredded longhorn cheese
1 cup cooking oil
1 cup guacamole
½ cup salsa or picante sauce
1 cup chopped lettuce
½ cup chopped tomato

In a skillet with hot oil, dip tortillas to soften. Place a small amount of roast beef and cheese across each tortilla. Roll tightly and secure with toothpicks. Fry in hot oil until tortillas are browned and crisp. Drain on paper towels. Serve 2 to a person with guacamole and salsa. Garnish with lettuce and tomato. 6 Servings.

Celebrate San Antonio
San Antonio Junior Forum, San Antonio, Texas

PEPPERED RIB EYE STEAK

1 rib eye (6- to 8-pound), fat removed
2 tablespoons oil
Salt
¼ to ½ can cracked or fresh ground pepper
1 onion, chopped
1 carrot, sliced
1 rib celery, chopped
½ cup red burgundy wine
1 can beef consommé

Rub meat with oil, salt, and pepper. The amount depends on taste. Spread onion, carrot and celery in a shallow pan. Place meat on top and roast uncovered at 350° for 15 minutes for each pound. Baste frequently with a mixture of wine and consommé. 12 to 14 Servings.

Lone Star Legacy
Austin Junior Forum, Inc., Austin, Texas

QUICK CHEESE STEAKS

2 tablespoons onion, grated
1 tablespoon shortening
4 to 6 cubed steaks
1 can tomato soup
1 teaspoon sugar
¼ teaspoon basil
1 teaspoon salt
¼ cup Parmesan cheese

Cook onion in melted shortening. Add steaks and fry until brown. Add other ingredients, except cheese. Put into a 2-quart casserole and cover tightly. (May freeze at this point. Cool first, then seal, and freeze. Thaw frozen steaks before baking.) Bake in a preheated 350° oven for 55 minutes or until steaks are tender. Sprinkle with Parmesan cheese and bake 5 more minutes. 4 to 6 Servings.

Simply Sensational
TWIGS, The Children's Medical Center, Dayton, Ohio

RARE ROAST BEEF

Beef roast up to 10-pounds, rump or sirloin tip
1 clove garlic
5 teaspoons kosher salt (regular salt may be used, but isn't as good as kosher)

In a small bowl, put garlic through a press and mix with salt. Rub mixture on each end and on exposed fat. Cook at 190° to 200° 1 hour per pound for roasts under 4-pounds or ¾ hour per pound for roasts over 4-pounds. Do not open oven door until ready to test for doneness. Do not baste or turn. The roast should be rare at the appointed time. If necessary it may stay in oven 1 more hour and still be rare. Use a meat thermometer to double check your time. There can be a difference between individual ovens. There will be no gravy in the pan because all juice stays in the roast. Make your own gravy or use an au jus mix. 8 to 10 Servings.

Talk About Good II

Junior League of Lafayette, Inc., Lafayette, Louisiana

SAUERBRATEN

2 onions, sliced
2 bay leaves
1 teaspoon black peppercorns
1 clove garlic, crushed
1 cup lemon juice
2½ cups water
½ cup sugar
4 pound rump roast
Cooking oil
12 gingersnap cookies, crushed

Combine and heat all ingredients except roast and cookies. Pour mixture over meat and marinate 24 to 36 hours, turning meat occasionally. Remove meat and wipe dry. Brown in hot oil. Add marinade, cover and simmer in 325° oven for 2 hours or until tender. To make gravy, combine ¾ cup strained marinade, ¼ cup water and gingersnaps. Cook until thickened. 4 to 6 Servings.

Talk About Good II
Junior League of Lafayette, Inc., Lafayette, Louisiana

SIRLOIN TIP ROAST

Cooked on the Grill

⅓ cup wine vinegar
⅓ cup red wine
3 tablespoons soy sauce
⅓ cup Worcestershire sauce
¼ cup olive oil
1 onion, chopped
Salt and pepper to taste
Garlic salt to taste
5 pounds sirloin tip, tied to fix on rotisserie

Mix all ingredients and marinate roast overnight in the marinade. Heat fire to at least 600° on the grill. Cook the roast 20 to 25 minutes per pound. A 5-pound roast cooks in 1½ to 2 hours. Delicious! 6 to 8 Servings.

Party Potpourri

Junior League of Memphis, Inc., Memphis, Tennessee

SPANISH STEAK

1½ pounds round steak
¾ teaspoon salt
½ teaspoon cracked pepper
1 teaspoon Worcestershire sauce
1 small onion
½ green pepper, chopped
1 small can mushrooms
2 (8-ounce) cans tomato sauce
2 teaspoons lemon juice

Put beef in large iron skillet, sprinkle with salt, pepper and Worcestershire. Slice onion and place vegetables on top of meat. Pour tomato juice and lemon juice over all. Bake five minutes in 400° oven, reduce temperature to 325° and bake 1 to 1½ hours. If tomato sauce gets too thick, add 1 to 2 tablespoonfuls boiling water. 4 Servings.

Recipe Jubilee
Junior League of Mobile, Inc., Mobile, Alabama

SPICY FLANK STEAK

½ cup catsup
½ cup water
¼ cup lemon juice
2 teaspoons Worcestershire sauce
1 bay leaf
1 teaspoon pepper
¼ teaspoon celery seeds
Dash of hot pepper sauce
2 to 3 pound flank steak

Combine all ingredients except steak. Simmer over low heat for 10 minutes. Cool. Marinate flank steak 8 to 24 hours. Grill over medium heat for 8 to 10 minutes. 4 Servings.

Riverfeast
Junior League of Cincinnati, Ohio

SPICY POT ROAST

4 to 5 pound beef pot roast
¼ cup shortening
3 cups water
1 cup vinegar
½ cup firmly packed brown sugar
½ cup chopped onion
2 tablespoons mixed pickling spices
2 tablespoons cardamom seed
⅓ cup flour
⅓ cup cold water

Brown meat slowly on all sides in shortening. Pour off excess fat; add next 6 ingredients. Simmer, covered 3 to 4 hours, or until meat is tender. Remove meat, keep warm. Strain stock, measure 4 cups. Blend flour and cold water; add to measured stock and cook, stirring until thickened. 8 Servings.

Woman's Exchange Cookbook, Volume II
Woman's Exchange of Memphis, Inc., Memphis, Tennessee

STEAK PIQUANTE

*Children may not particularly care for this,
but adults most certainly do!*

⅛ to ¼ pound blue or Roquefort cheese
3 teaspoons butter
4 tablespoons steak sauce
4 tablespoons Worcestershire sauce
Dash hot pepper sauce
4 teaspoons catsup
2 teaspoons prepared mustard
4 servings steak, T-bone or sirloin

Mix ingredients. Broil steak in oven or outside on grill. After steak has been turned to cook on second side, coat top with sauce. You may wish to season steak with salt and pepper as usual. A blender mixes the sauce smoothly, but is not essential.

Cotton Country Cooking
Decatur Junior Service League, Inc., Decatur, Alabama

SUNDAY DINNER ROAST BEEF

4 pounds eye of the round roast
Salt to taste
Pepper to taste
Crab apples, optional
Parsley, optional

Have roast at room temperature. Season with salt and pepper. Preheat oven to 500° until light goes off. Bake roast 8 minutes per pound. Turn oven off and do not open door until cool, about 2½ hours. Slice, arrange on platter, and garnish with apples and parsley. This is excellent for Sunday dinner as it will finish cooking while the cook is at church with no fear of the roast burning. 8 Servings.

Land of Cotton
John T. Morgan Academy, Selma, Alabama

SWISS STEAK FOR TWO

¾ pound beef round steak, ½ to ¾-inch thick
2 tablespoons flour
¼ teaspoon salt
½ teaspoon pepper
2 tablespoons salad oil
1 (8-ounce) can stewed tomatoes
1 medium green pepper, sliced
1 medium onion, sliced
½ teaspoon salt

Cut meat into two slices. Mix flour, salt, and pepper; coat meat. Heat oil in 8-inch skillet and brown meat over medium heat about 15 minutes. Add tomatoes. Reduce heat, cover, and simmer 30 minutes. Add green pepper, onion, and salt. cover and simmer until meat is tender, about 30 to 45 minutes. Add water if necessary.

The Pick of the Crop
North Sunflower PTA, Drew, Mississippi

SYMPHONY BEEF

2 tablespoons butter
1 pint sour cream
14 ounces canned artichoke hearts
½ cup dry vermouth
1½ tablespoons Parmesan cheese
½ pound chipped beef
English muffins, buttered and toasted

Melt butter in skillet; add sour cream and stir until smooth. Slice artichoke hearts and add to sour cream. Add wine, cheese and chipped beef. Stir all together and keep warm. Serve over muffins. 4 Servings.

Virginia Hospitality
Junior League of Hampton Roads, Inc., Hampton, Virginia

TEXAS GRILL

5 to 7 pound sirloin tip roast or brisket
½ teaspoon garlic powder
½ cup salad oil
1 teaspoon cayenne (red) pepper
1 teaspoon paprika
1 cup tomato sauce
1 cup chili sauce
1 teaspoon oregano
1 tablespoon ground black pepper

Mix all ingredients for basting sauce. Place meat on grill, away from coals. Roast 3½ to 4 hours, basting generously every 30 minutes. Turn meat after each basting. Cook with lid closed. If meat thermometer is used, cook until 160°. Outside of meat will be crusty. Start to prepare early in the day. 10 to 12 Servings.

Simply Sensational
TWIGS, The Children's Medical Center, Dayton, Ohio

WAGONER'S GRILLED FLANK STEAK

Soy sauce
1 flank steak, tenderized
6 to 8 slices bacon

Sprinkle soy sauce over both sides of steak and set aside for at least 1 hour. Fry bacon and drain well. Place bacon strips crosswise over steak. Roll steak tightly and secure with skewers. Cut the roll into slices at least ½-inch thick. Grill to desired doneness. 4 to 6 Servings.

Deep in the Heart
Dallas Junior Forum, Inc., Dallas, Texas

PLANTERS' RIBS

3 to 4 pounds pork back ribs, or 7 to 8 ribs per person
2½ cups homemade barbecue sauce
½ cup firmly packed dark brown sugar

Parboil ribs in simmering water for 45 minutes; drain. Spread barbecue sauce over ribs and bake in a preheated 325° oven for 1½ hours. Sprinkle with brown sugar and bake or grill 30 minutes longer. 6 Servings.

Atlanta Cooknotes
Junior League of Atlanta, Inc., Atlanta, Georgia

POLYNESIAN RIBS

2 packages ribs
½ cup sugar
1 teaspoon hickory smoked salt
1 cup catsup
1 cup soy sauce
1 teaspoon ginger
2 tablespoons brown sugar
1 teaspoon monosodium glutamate (optional)

Rub ribs with sugar and hickory smoked salt; let stand for 1 hour. Combine the catsup, soy sauce, ginger, brown sugar, and monosodium glutamate (if desired); rub on ribs. Let them stand for 2 hours. Place in a preheated 400° oven. Reduce heat to 325° and cook until tender, about 40 minutes. Serve immediately. 4 Servings.

Southern Elegance
Junior League of Gaston County, North Carolina

SPANISH SPARE RIBS

2 whole heads of garlic
⅔ cup sweet orange juice
⅓ cup lime juice
3 teaspoons oregano
3 pounds pork spare ribs

Peel garlic and press into orange juice, lime juice and oregano. Pour all together over ribs and marinate 24 hours. Drain juice and reserve. Bake at 450° for at least 1 hour or cook on grill. As ribs cook, baste with juice frequently. The secret is in marinating for 24 hours and basting while cooking. 6 Servings.

Virginia Seasons
Junior League of Richmond, Virginia

SWEET AND SOUR SPARERIBS

2 pounds spareribs
1½ cups water
¼ cup raisins or currants
½ teaspoon salt
2 green peppers cut into ¾-inch strips
1½ tablespoons cornstarch
¼ cup sugar
¼ cup vinegar
¼ cup soy sauce

Cut ribs into serving portions and brown in fry pan over moderate heat about 5 minutes on each side. Add ½ cup water, raisins or currants and salt. Cover pan tightly and cook over low heat for 20 minutes. Add green peppers. Stir in cornstarch blended with sugar, vinegar and 1 cup water. Cover again and cook over low heat for 30 minutes, stirring occasionally. Add more water as needed to prevent drying. Before serving, add soy sauce. 3 to 4 Servings.

Cane River Cuisine

Service League of Natchitoches, Inc., Natchitoches, Louisiana

APPLE CREAM PORK CHOPS

2 (½-inch thick) pork chops
Salt and pepper
1 large tart apple
½ teaspoon celery salt
Vegetable oil
⅓ cup white wine or dry vermouth
⅓ cup whipping cream

Trim chops of fat. Sprinkle on both sides with salt and black pepper; pound lightly. Spread thinly sliced, quartered apple over bottom of shallow au gratin dish or casserole, 1 to 1½ inches deep. Sprinkle with the celery salt. Brown chops on both sides in very hot vegetable oil. Do not cook chops. Put chops on top of apple; pour in wine. Cover lightly with foil and bake at 350° for 45 minutes. Remove foil, pour the heavy cream over the chops and bake 15 to 20 minutes more. 2 Servings.

The Mount Vernon Cookbook
The Mount Vernon Ladies' Association of the Union, Mount Vernon, Virginia

BACON-WRAPPED PORK CHOPS

4 pork chops
4 slices bacon
½ cup soy sauce
2 tablespoons grated onion
1 tablespoon vinegar
½ teaspoon sugar
⅛ teaspoon cayenne
1 clove garlic, crushed

Wrap each chop with 1 slice of bacon, securing with toothpick. Place chops in 2-quart shallow casserole in single layer. Combine remaining ingredients; pour over chops. Cover. Bake at 325° for 1 to 1½ hours; turn once and remove cover after 40 minutes. 4 Servings.

Perennials
Junior Service League of Gainesville, Georgia, Inc.

BETTY'S BARBECUE PORK

For Sandwiches

4 to 6 pound pork loin roast
3 tablespoons brown sugar
1 cup vinegar
½ cup Worcestershire sauce
1 large onion, chopped
3 tablespoons prepared mustard
¼ teaspoon pepper
1½ cups ketchup

Pour all ingredients over pork roast in a Dutch oven and cook covered over low heat for 4 to 5 hours. Break up large pieces and remove bones if any. Serve in sandwich buns. Yield: 25 to 30 Sandwiches.

Georgia On My Menu
Junior League of Cobb-Marietta, Inc., Marietta, Georgia

CREOLE PORK CHOPS

6 pork chops
6 lemon slices, thin
6 onion slices, thin
6 teaspoons dark brown sugar
½ cup catsup
½ cup water

In a large skillet, brown pork chops on both sides. On each chop place a lemon slice, an onion slice and 1 teaspoon brown sugar. In a small bowl, combine catsup and water and mix. Pour over chops. Cook covered 1 hour over low heat until chops are cooked. 6 Servings.

Celebrate San Antonio
San Antonio Junior Forum, San Antonio, Texas

LEMON BARBECUE PORK CHOPS

2 tablespoons chopped green onion
1 tablespoon oleo
½ cup catsup
¼ cup soy sauce
Grated peel and juice of 1 lemon
2 tablespoons brown sugar
2 tablespoons white wine
6 pork chops, cut 1-inch thick

In small saucepan, sauté onion in butter. Stir in remaining ingredients, except pork chops. Simmer several minutes to blend. Cook pork chops in small amount of water 10 to 15 minutes. Drain and place on charcoal grill over hot coals. Cook 10 minutes and turn. Cook 5 minutes. Brush with sauce and continue cooking, 30 minutes, turning every 10 minutes and basting.

The Pick of the Crop
North Sunflower PTA, Drew, Mississippi

NOT JUST PORK CHOPS

This just must be done to taste so try it on your family before guests. But good enough for any company meal.

3 tablespoons to ¼ cup soy sauce
½ to ¾ cup light brown sugar
½ lime, sliced thin
2 green onions, chopped with tops
Juice of ½ lime
1 teaspoon grated lime peel

Marinate pork chops for about 30 minutes in refrigerator. Brown in hot skillet (without grease) very briefly. They brown well because of the marinade but can burn if you aren't careful. Place lime slices on top of pork chops. Add a little water to marinade, pour over chops and bake at 325° until tender. Serve with fluffy rice.

Talk About Good
Junior League of Lafayette, Inc., Lafayette, Louisiana

OVEN BARBECUED PORK CHOPS

6 pork chops
½ cup ketchup
1 teaspoon celery seed
1 bay leaf
2 tablespoons brown sugar
4 tablespoons white vinegar
1 cup water
1 teaspoon prepared mustard

Brown pork chops. Arrange in bottom of a shallow baking pan so they do not overlap. While chops are browning, mix all other ingredients in small saucepan and heat. Pour over chops and bake uncovered at 375° for 1 hour. Check after 45 minutes to see that sauce is not getting too thick. If so, cover for remaining 15 minutes.

Rare Collection
Junior League of Galveston County, Texas, Inc.

PORK CHOPS AND ORANGE SAUCE

4 pork chops (1-inch thick)
Seasoned salt
4 tablespoons water
5 tablespoons sugar
1½ teaspoons cornstarch
Dash of salt
¼ teaspoon cinnamon
10 whole cloves
1 to 2 teaspoons grated orange rind
½ cup orange juice
4 orange slices

Brown pork chops. Sprinkle with seasoned salt. Add water, cover, and simmer 1 hour or until tender. Drain any remaining water. Make syrup separately of remaining ingredients, boiling until clear and slightly thickened. Pour over pork chops. 4 Servings.

Deep in the Heart
Dallas Junior Forum, Inc,. Dallas, Texas

PORK GRILL

2-pounds lean pork, cubed, or 2-pounds thick chops (large for entrée, small for appetizer)
6 Brazil nuts, grated (optional)
2 garlic cloves, crushed
½ cup soy sauce
1 tablespoon honey or 2 tablespoons brown sugar
½ cup olive oil
¼ cup lemon juice
1 tablespoon curry powder
1 tablespoon chili powder
1 cup minced onion

Marinate pork in sauce for at least 1 hour or overnight. Thread pork on skewers and bake in hot oven (450°) for 20 minutes or over medium fire on grill. Grill thick chops for about 40 to 60 minutes. 6 Servings.

CordonBluegrass
Junior League of Louisville, Inc., Louisville, Kentucky

PORK ROAST WITH RICE

3 to 5 pounds pork roast
1 to 2 quarts hot water
2 cups rice, uncooked
1 cup onions or scallions, chopped
1 can mushrooms, chopped
½ cup green pepper, chopped
Salt and pepper to taste

Place roast, seasoned to taste, on rack of roaster pan, fat side up, untrimmed. Pour water in bottom of roaster. All the meat seasoning and drippings will be in the liquid. Bake in 350° oven until done, about 3½ hours. One hour before roast is done, add rice to liquid in pan. Add more water, as rice will absorb the liquid. 20 to 30 minutes before rice is done, add remaining ingredients and stir into rice. Keep the rice moist and shiny in appearance. Rice and roast will be ready at the same time. 4 to 5 Servings.

Woman's Exchange Cookbook, Volume II
Woman's Exchange of Memphis, Tennessee

SOUR CREAM PORK CHOPS

6 (1-inch) pork chops
1 clove garlic
4 tablespoons shortening
½ pint sour cream
1 tablespoon vinegar
1 tablespoon Worcestershire sauce
½ teaspoon salt
¼ teaspoon pepper
½ teaspoon paprika
3 bay leaves
Minced parsley

Rub pork chops with garlic and brown in shortening. Mix sour cream with next 5 ingredients. Pour over meat and place ½ bay leaf on each chop. Sprinkle with parsley. Bake at 350° for 40 minutes. Flavor is enhanced when prepared in the morning for dinner.

Seasoned With Sun
Junior League of El Paso, Inc. El Paso, Texas

ATLANTA BAKED HAM

1 (7-pound) half or whole ham
2 tablespoons prepared mustard
⅓ cup firmly packed brown sugar
2 tablespoons peanut butter
1 teaspoon horseradish
18 to 20 whole cloves
½ cup cola-flavored soda

Preheat oven to 325°. Bake ham 25 minutes per pound for a half ham, or slightly less for a whole ham. Combine mustard, brown sugar, peanut butter, and horseradish, mixing well. Set aside. When about 45 minutes baking time remain, remove ham from oven. Trim off rind and fat; pour excess fat from pan. Stud top of ham with cloves, and spread with mustard sauce. Pour cola in pan and return ham to oven, basting several times with pan juices. 8 to 10 Servings.

Atlanta Cooknotes
Junior League of Atlanta, Inc., Atlanta, Georgia

FRESH HAM MARSALA

12 pound fresh ham
Vinegar
2 cloves garlic, crushed
1 bottle Marsala wine
1 cup water
Brown sugar

Rub ham with vinegar and garlic cloves. Place in a casserole and pour 1 bottle of Marsala over it. Add water and sprinkle with brown sugar. Wrap ham in foil and cook in a slow oven (325°) 25 minutes per pound. 8 Servings.

The Mount Vernon Cookbook
The Mount Vernon Ladies' Association of the Union, Mount Vernon, Virginia

FRESH PORK HAM

1 (5- to 8-pound) fresh pork ham
Slivers of garlic
1 bell pepper
Salt, red and black pepper
1 small onion
Parsley

Cut excess fat from ham and remove thick skin. With sharp knife, cut 5 or 6 deep slits in meat and fill each with salt, pepper and a sliver each of garlic, onion and bell pepper. Season entire outside. Place in shallow pan, fat side up, and roast in 325° over for 30 to 35 minutes per pound. When done, remove roast but do not carve for at least 15 minutes. Pour off some of the drippings, and over low heat stir in a little flour and add some water to make gravy. Season gravy to taste. Cut up some parsley in the gravy. Good served with rice and a spinach casserole.

Talk About Good
Junior League of Lafayette, Inc., Lafayette, Louisiana

GEORGIA COUNTRY HAM

1 (10- to 12-pound) Georgia country ham
1 cup brown sugar
1 cup bourbon or sherry
1 cup water

Have the hock cut off ham so that it will fit into a roaster. Soak ham overnight in cold water and scrub the ham with a stiff brush. Change water a couple of times to get rid of the excess salt. Mix sugar, bourbon and water; press into the fat of ham. Cover tightly with foil in roaster and bake at 200° for 8 hours. 12 Servings.

Savannah Style
Junior League of Savannah, Inc., Savannah, Georgia

SWEDISH HAM BALLS IN BROWN SAUCE

1 pound ground ham
1½ pounds ground pork
2 cups bread crumbs
2 eggs, well beaten
1 cup milk

1 cup brown sugar
1 teaspoon dry mustard
½ cup vinegar
½ cup water

Combine meats, crumbs, eggs and milk, mixing well. Form into balls and place in pan. Combine remaining ingredients and stir until sugar dissolves. Pour over meat balls and bake for 1 hour in 325° oven, basting frequently. Yield: 16 Balls.

Recipe Jubilee
Junior League of Mobile, Inc., Mobile, Alabama

SPICY PORK LOIN

5 large cloves fresh garlic, minced
2 teaspoons paprika
¼ cup crushed peppercorns
1 teaspoon ground red pepper
½ cup vegetable oil
4 pound boneless center cut pork loin roast

In small bowl, combine seasonings. Add oil and rub mixture over pork. Cover with plastic wrap and refrigerate overnight. Use covered kettle grill. Arrange coals in a circle; put a drip pan beneath roast. Grill, turning roast occasionally until temperature of meat reaches 170°, approximately 2 hours. Let stand 10 minutes. 6 Servings.

Riverfeast
Junior League of Cincinnati, Ohio

Pork Loin In Milk

3 tablespoons oil
4 tablespoons butter
4 to 5 pounds boneless pork roast
1 tablespoon salt
1 teaspoon pepper
1 teaspoon paprika
1 bay leaf
5 cups milk
1 cup white wine
1 teaspoon rosemary

Heat the oil and 3 tablespoons of butter in a casserole. Brown the roast on all sides. Add salt, pepper, paprika and bay leaf and a little milk. Allow milk to caramelize. Pour the rest of the milk over the roast. Reduce heat and allow to simmer for 2 hours. The milk will turn brown. Remove roast and make sauce by reducing milk by ½ in casserole; then add the wine, rosemary and the rest of the butter. Allow sauce to thicken. Serve with the roast.

A Taste of New England
Junior League of Worcester, Inc., Worcester, Massachusetts

HOPPING JOHN

8 slices slab bacon, cut into pieces
2 small onions, chopped
5 cups canned black eyed peas, including juice
1 cup uncooked pork, cubed
2½ cups water
1 cup rice, uncooked
⅛ teaspoon cayenne
Salt to taste

Sauté bacon and onions until onions are tender. Remove from pan. Cook pork in the bacon drippings until lightly browned. Add other ingredients to pan and cook over medium heat about 25 minutes. Serve on New Year's Day for good luck all year! 6 to 8 Servings.

Virginia Hospitality
Junior League of Hampton Roads, Inc., Hampton, Virginia

PORK TENDERLOIN IN CURRANT SAUCE

2 pounds pork tenderloin
2 tablespoons butter
1½ teaspoons salt
½ teaspoon pepper
½ teaspoon rosemary
4 tablespoons butter or margarine
½ cup currant jelly
½ to 1 cup light cream
3 tablespoons flour

Salt and pepper the whole tenderloin and brown in butter. Place in casserole and sprinkle with rosemary. Spread with butter and top with currant jelly. Cover and bake at 325°, for about 35 minutes per pound. Blend flour and cream and stir into the liquid. Bake an additional 10 minutes. On a platter slice into pieces about ⅜-inch thick and overlap on individual plates. Spoon about 2 to 3 tablespoons of sauce on each serving and serve the remainder in a small pitcher. 6 Servings.

A Taste of New England
Junior League of Worcester, Inc., Worcester, Massachusetts

BARBECUED FRANKFURTERS

3 medium onions
6 tablespoons vinegar
3 tablespoons flour
4½ tablespoons Worcestershire sauce
2 tablespoons salt
3 pinches red pepper
1 tablespoon paprika
¾ teaspoon black pepper
1 tablespoon chili powder or dry mustard
1½ cups tomato catsup
2 tablespoons brown sugar
6 tablespoons hot water
20 to 25 frankfurters
Hot dog buns

Chop onions; blend vinegar and flour and combine with onions, seasonings, sugar, and water. Pierce each frank 5 or 6 times with a fork and dip into sauce. Arrange franks in well greased roaster and pour remaining sauce over them. Cover and bake 1 hour at 350°. Serve from roaster putting frank and some sauce in each hot dog bun.

Party Potpourri
Junior League of Memphis, Inc., Memphis, Tennessee

BEEF FAJITAS

¼ cup soy sauce
¼ cup tequila
3 cloves garlic, minced
¼ cup extra virgin olive oil
1½ pounds skirt steak
Flour tortillas, warmed
2 tomatoes, chopped
1 large onion, sliced and grilled
1 avocado, sliced
Sour cream

Marinate steak overnight in soy sauce, tequila, garlic and oil. Cook on barbecue and baste with marinade; grill to your taste. Slice at a 45° angle into thin strips. Serve in tortillas and top with tomatoes, onions, avocado and sour cream. Serve picante sauce with the fajitas. 6 Servings.

A Touch of Atlanta
Marist School, Atlanta, Georgia

BEEF STROGANOFF

2 pounds round steak
¼ cup flour
Dash black pepper
¼ cup butter
½ pound mushrooms, sliced
1½ cans consommé, undiluted
1½ tablespoons chopped parsley
1 cup sour cream

Cut round steak into thin strips, dust with flour and pepper, brown in butter. Add mushrooms, consommé and parsley. Cook gently, covered, for 1 hour, or until meat is tender. Before serving, blend in sour cream. Simmer for 5 minutes. Serve over noodles or rice. 6 Servings.

Woman's Exchange Cookbook, Volume II
Woman's Exchange of Memphis, Inc., Memphis, Tennessee

BURGUNDY BURGERS

1 pound ground chuck
⅔ cup dry bread crumbs
⅓ cup dry red wine (Burgundy suggested)
3 tablespoons chili sauce
1 tablespoon instant minced onion
1 teaspoon horseradish
1 teaspoon Dijon mustard
1 teaspoon Worcestershire sauce
½ teaspoon salt
⅛ teaspoon garlic powder
¼ teaspoon pepper
2 English muffins, split, toasted, and buttered

Combine all ingredients except English muffins in a medium size bowl. Shape into 4 patties. Grill 4-inches from hot coals for about 6 minutes on each side for medium doneness. Serve on English muffin half. 4 Servings.

Simply Sensational
TWIGS, The Children's Medical Center, Dayton, Ohio

CHILE VERDE

3 large pork chops, cut into ¼-inch strips
¼ cup flour
¼ cup oil
2 (7-ounce) cans chopped green chiles
1 medium yellow onion, chopped
1 (10-ounce) can red salsa
1 to 3 cloves garlic, minced
Salt and pepper to taste
Rice or flour tortillas
Sour cream
Cilantro
Black olives

Coat pork cubes with flour. Brown in oil in a large heavy skillet, add seasonings, chiles, chopped onion and salsa. If necessary, add water, cover and simmer about 45 minutes, again adding water if necessary. Serve over rice or in heated flour tortillas with condiments such as sour cream, cilantro, and black olives. 4 to 6 Servings. (Can also be served as hors d'oeuvres with sturdy tortilla chips.)

Only in California
Children's Home Society of California, Los Angeles, California

CHINESE BEEF AND RADISHES

1½ pounds thinly sliced beef
2 tablespoons cornstarch
4 tablespoons soy sauce
8 tablespoons water
6 tablespoons oil
⅔ cup white vinegar
1 cup sugar
2 cups red radishes, thinly sliced
1 cup chopped scallions
White rice

Marinate beef in cornstarch, soy sauce and water. Heat 6 tablespoons oil in frying pan. Add vinegar and sugar and heat to boiling point. Lower heat and add radishes. When radishes are almost transparent, add scallions. Add beef and stir until just cooked. Serve over rice. 6 Servings.

RSVP
Junior League of Portland, Maine, Inc.

CORNED BEEF

1 fancy corned brisket of beef
½ large onion, sliced
1 bay leaf
3 carrots, peeled and halved
½ stalk celery
3 whole cloves

Place corned beef in kettle and cover with cold water. Add other ingredients. Bring to a boil. Cover and simmer 3½ to 5 hours or until tender. The corned beef is best when refrigerated and then sliced into exceedingly thin slices. Serve with mustard, Swiss cheese, and cabbage, cooked in the stock.

Recipe Jubilee
Junior League of Mobile, Inc., Mobile, Alabama

FRUIT GLAZED CORNED BEEF

6 pounds corned beef brisket
½ cup brown sugar
2 teaspoons orange peel, grated
½ teaspoon dry mustard
½ cup apple cider
⅓ cup orange juice
2 tablespoons fresh lemon juice

Combine sugar, orange and lemon peel and mustard; pat onto meat. Combine juices and pour over meat. Bake uncovered at 350° for 1 hour, basting occasionally. 6 Servings.

A Touch of Atlanta
Marist School, Atlanta, Georgia

GRANDMOTHER MUSKIE'S POLISH MEATLOAF

2 pounds ground chuck
2 cups bread cubes
1 egg
½ cup milk
1 medium onion, chopped
Salt and pepper, to taste

In large bowl, mix all ingredients. Make two large patties and brown in hot skillet. When very brown on both sides, lower heat; add 1-inch water to pan and simmer for 1 hour. Keep adding small amounts of water while cooking; make your favorite gravy with pan liquid. Pour gravy over meat and serve immediately. 4 to 5 Servings.

RSVP
Junior League of Portland, Maine, Inc.

ITALIAN SAUSAGES, BLACK AND GREEN

1 bunch broccoli
1½ pounds sausage
1 glass dry white wine
4 tablespoons olive oil
1 tablespoon oregano
1 pinch dry hot pepper
3 cloves garlic, minced
1 can black Italian olives, drained

Wash broccoli, cut flowers apart, skin and quarter stems. Cook in boiling salted water for 3 minutes. Drain and set aside. Sauté sausage in a skillet over medium heat. When cooked, drain off excess fat and add wine, olive oil, and seasonings. Then add cooked broccoli and olives. Simmer for 20 minutes. Add warm water when needed. 6 Servings.

Party Potpourri
Junior League of Memphis, Inc., Memphis, Tennessee

MEATBALLS

1 pound ground beef
2 eggs, beaten
2 tablespoons chopped parsley
2 tablespoons Parmesan cheese
½ cup seasoned bread crumbs
1 garlic clove, minced
1½ teaspoons salt
⅛ teaspoon pepper
2 tablespoons vegetable oil

Mix all ingredients and form into balls. Fry in oil and drain on paper. Add to your favorite sauce. 8 Servings.

Riverfeast
Junior League of Cincinnati, Ohio

PARSLEY STEAK ROLLS

1 large round steak
1 (4-ounce) can mushrooms, drained
1 onion, finely chopped
3 teaspoons Parmesan cheese
Salt and pepper to taste
Dry parsley flakes
1 teaspoon cornstarch
1 (10½-ounce) can beef broth

Place mushrooms, finely chopped onions, cheese, salt, pepper and parsley flakes on round steak. Roll into large roll. Secure with toothpicks or heavy string. Or, you may cut steak into individual serving sizes, season, then roll and secure. Brown in hot fat on all sides. Stir cornstarch into small amount of broth. Add to remaining broth. Pour over steak rolls. Cover. Cook at 350° for 1 hour. 5 to 6 Servings.

Southern Accent
Junior League of Pine Bluff, Inc., Pine Bluff, Arkansas

PIGS IN A BLANKET

1 (4- to 4½-pound) beef sirloin, sliced as thinly as possible
1 cup finely chopped onion
2 pounds finely chopped bacon
Toothpicks
3 tablespoons oil
6 cups water
Salt and pepper to taste
½ teaspoon browning sauce
3 tablespoons flour

Pound slices of meat. Combine onion and bacon. Place approximately 2 heaping tablespoons in the middle of each slice of meat, roll and secure either end with toothpicks. Brown rolls in oils. Add 6 cups of water. Season with salt and pepper and ½ teaspoon browning sauce. Simmer for ½ hour. Dissolve flour in small amount of water and add to gravy to thicken. Simmer 10 minutes more. 6 Servings.

Talk About Good II

Junior League of Lafayette, Inc., Lafayette, Louisiana

RIO GRANDE SUPPER

3½ pounds corned beef brisket
2 medium cloves garlic
2 teaspoons whole peppercorns
6 small white onions, peeled
6 carrots, peeled
1 medium head cabbage, halved
6 to 8 medium potatoes

Cover brisket in water. Add garlic and peppercorns and simmer over low heat 4½ hours. Add onions and continue simmering. In 20 to 25 minutes, add carrots. Cook 30 minutes; add cabbage. In 15 minutes, add potatoes. Simmer until potatoes are tender. Remove brisket and cool. Slice thinly. Serve on large platter surrounded by vegetables. Good with mustard and horseradish. 6 to 7 Servings.

Seasoned With Sun
Junior League of El Paso, Inc. El Paso, Texas

SLOW COOKING GOULASH

2 pounds boneless beef chuck, cut into 1-inch cubes (venison may be substituted for beef)
2 tablespoons all-purpose flour
1 small onion, diced
½ teaspoon garlic powder (optional)
1 teaspoon salt
1 teaspoon paprika
⅛ teaspoon pepper
1 (15-ounce) can tomato sauce
1 cup fresh or canned sliced mushrooms
½ cup sour cream

Place meat in a slow cook pot; add flour and toss until meat is coated. Add onion, optional garlic powder, salt, paprika, pepper and tomato sauce. Cook on low heat 6 to 10 hours or until meat is tender. Beef may also be cooked in a covered 3-quart casserole in a preheated 350° oven for 3 hours. Twenty minutes before serving, add mushrooms and sour cream. Serve over rice or in avocado halves. 6 to 8 Servings.

Atlanta Cooknotes
Junior League of Atlanta, Inc., Atlanta, Georgia

TACO MEAT LOAF

1½ pounds ground beef
1 cup crushed corn chips
⅓ cup taco sauce
1 tablespoon taco seasoning mix
1 egg, beaten
1 cup shredded cheese

Mix all ingredients. Bake in a loaf pan which has been lined with foil, if desired. Cook at 350° about 1 hour. Take out, drain off fat and put in oven for a minute or two longer. 6 Servings.

Southern Accent
Junior League of Pine Bluff, Inc., Pine Bluff, Arkansas

WORCESTER MEATLOAF

1 pound hamburger
1 egg
1 small onion, chopped
Garlic powder
1 teaspoon Worcestershire sauce
1 teaspoon ketchup
1 (16-ounce) can tomato sauce
¾ cup bread crumbs
½ pound mozzarella cheese, sliced

Mix all ingredients with ½ can tomato sauce. Spread out on waxed paper. Spread mozzarella slices on top and roll like a jelly roll. Bake 40 to 45 minutes at 350°. Pour remaining ½ can tomato sauce over top and bake 15 to 20 minutes more.

A Taste of New England
Junior League of Worcester, Inc., Worcester, Massachusetts

CELEBRATION LAMB CHOPS

So Simple

6 (1½-inch) loin lamb chops
Lemon juice
Minced garlic
Oregano
Black pepper

Coat one side of each lamb chop with following ingredients in the following order: lemon juice, garlic, oregano, and pepper. Place chops on broiling pan or grill with seasoned side to heat. Season other side the same way. Cook 8 minutes per side for medium rare. Turn once.

Rare Collection
Junior League of Galveston County, Texas, Inc.

ITALIAN VEAL ROAST

1 (3-pound) boneless veal roast
3 tablespoons extra virgin olive oil
1 (28-ounce) can crushed tomatoes
1 red bell pepper, sliced
½ white onion, sliced
⅛ teaspoon oregano
⅛ teaspoon basil
1 garlic clove, minced
Salt and pepper, to taste
Grated mozzarella cheese

Brown veal in hot oil. Add remaining ingredients, cover and cook over low heat for 1½ hours. Remove roast, slice and cover with the sauce. If desired, sprinkle grated mozzarella cheese over the sauce and heat until cheese is melted. 6 Servings.

A Touch of Atlanta
Marist School, Atlanta, Georgia

PEPPERY VEAL

1 to 1½ pounds veal chops, the equivalent of a beef T-bone
¼ cup flour
¼ cup vegetable oil
Salt
Lots of fresh ground black pepper

Very lightly flour veal. Shake off any excess flour. Dip veal into fresh ground black pepper. Gently rub in pepper. Heat the oil in a large, heavy skillet. Sauté the veal for 2 minutes on each side. Salt to taste. Serve hot. 2 to 4 Servings.

The Wild Wild West
The Junior League of Odessa, Inc., Odessa, Texas

GRILLADES

1 round steak
Salt and pepper
3 tablespoons flour
3 tablespoons shortening or oil
1 large onion, chopped
2 tomatoes, chopped
1½ to 2 cups water
½ teaspoon vinegar

Pound round steak well and cut into 4-inch pieces. Salt and pepper well and dust lightly with flour. Brown in shortening, remove and set aside. In the same skillet, make a roux of flour and shortening. Add chopped onion, tomatoes and their juice, water and vinegar. Place browned steak on top. Cover and simmer slowly for 45 minutes to 1 hour. Very nice with grits for a morning brunch. 4 Servings.

Cane River Cuisine
Service League of Natchitoches, Inc., Natchitoches, Louisiana

PEKING HAMBURGERS

½ pound ground beef
1 (8½-ounce) can sliced pineapple
3 tablespoons brown sugar
1 teaspoon cornstarch
1½ tablespoons red wine vinegar
1½ teaspoons soy sauce
1½ teaspoons Worcestershire sauce

Shape ground beef into 2 patties. Brown over medium heat 3 minutes on each side. Drain pineapple, reserving 2 tablespoons syrup, Combine remaining ingredients, including reserved syrup. Heat with pineapple slices in separate saucepan, stirring occasionally until sauce thickens. Place pineapple slices on burgers; spoon sauce over. 2 Servings.

Perennials
Junior Service League of Gainesville, Georgia, Inc.

SHEPHERD'S PIE

A child's do-it-yourself favorite!

1 pound ground beef
½ teaspoon garlic powder
½ teaspoon onion powder or finely chopped onion
2 teaspoons chili powder
Salt and pepper
1 (1-pound) can whole tomatoes
2 cups cooked instant mashed potatoes
Grated cheese, optional

Brown meat; add seasonings and tomatoes. Cook until tomatoes are mixed in well. Cook potatoes by package directions. Place meat mixture in casserole, top with potatoes and sprinkle with cheese. Bake at 350° until brown.

Southern Accent
Junior League of Pine Bluff, Inc., Pine Bluff, Arkansas

J-B RANCH CASSEROLE

2 pounds ground meat
2 cloves garlic, minced
Salt and pepper, to taste
½ medium onion, chopped
½ medium bell pepper, chopped
2 tablespoons barbecue sauce
1 tablespoon Worcestershire sauce
1 (16-ounce) can ranch-style beans
⅓ cup cooked white rice
½ cup processed cheese, grated

Add garlic, salt and pepper to meat and mix well. In large skillet, cook meat with onions and bell pepper until done. Add barbecue sauce, Worcestershire sauce and beans. Simmer about 5 minutes. Stir in cooked rice. Pour into a casserole dish and top with grated cheese. Bake in a preheated 350° oven until bubbly and cheese is melted. 8 Servings.

The Wild Wild West
The Junior League of Odessa, Inc., Odessa, Texas

24 HOUR MEAT MARINADE

2 cups olive oil
½ cup tarragon vinegar
1 clove garlic, chopped
1½ teaspoons salt
1½ teaspoons pepper
½ teaspoon curry powder
2 bay leaves
½ teaspoon lemon juice
3 dashes hot pepper sauce

In a large mixing bowl, combine olive oil, vinegar, garlic, salt, pepper, curry powder, bay leaves, lemon juice and hot pepper sauce. Mix well and use as a 24 hour marinade on beef. Barbecue, stir fry or oven bake as desired. Yield: 4 cups.

Celebrate San Antonio
San Antonio Junior Forum, San Antonio, Texas

ACKNOWLEDGMENTS

The publisher wishes to thank the following organizations for participating in the series. To order the following cookbooks, please contact the publishing organization directly.

ATLANTA COOKNOTES
Junior League of Atlanta, Inc.
P.O. Box 53428
Atlanta, GA 30355-1428

CANE RIVER CUISINE
Service League of Natchitoches, Inc.
P.O. Box 2206
Natchitoches, LA 71457

CELEBRATE SAN ANTONIO
San Antonio Junior Forum
P.O. Box 791186
San Antonio, TX 78279-1186

CORDONBLUEGRASS
Junior League of Louisville, Inc.
627 W. Main St., Dept. R99
Louisville, KY 40202

COTTON COUNTRY COOKING
Decatur Junior Service League, Inc.
P.O. Box 486
Decatur, AL 35602

DEEP IN THE HEART
Dallas Junior Forum, Inc.
800 E. Campbell, Suite 199
Richardson, TX 75081

GEORGIA ON MY MENU
Junior League of Cobb-Marietta, Inc.
P.O. Box 727
Marietta, GA 30060

LAND OF COTTON
John T. Morgan Academy
P.O. Drawer P
Selma, AL 36702

LONE STAR LEGACY
Austin Junior Forum, Inc.
P.O. Box 26628
Austin, TX 78755-0628

ACKNOWLEDGMENTS

THE MOUNT VERNON COOKBOOK
The Mount Vernon Ladies' Association of the Union
Mount Vernon, VA 22121

ONLY IN CALIFORNIA
Children's Home Society of California
2727 W. 6th St.
Los Angeles, CA 90057-3111

PARTY POTPOURRI
Junior League of Memphis, Inc.
2711 Union Avenue, Extended
Memphis, TN 38112

PERENNIALS
Junior Service League of Gainesville, Georgia, Inc.
P.O. Box 32
Gainesville, GA 30503

THE PICK OF THE CROP
North Sunflower PTA
Route 2, Box 821
Drew, MS 38737

RARE COLLECTION
Junior League of Galveston County, Inc.
210 Kempner St.
Galveston, TX 77550

RECIPE JUBILEE
Junior League of Mobile, Inc.
P.O. Box 7091, Mobile, AL 36607

RIVERFEAST
Junior League of Cincinnati
3500 Columbia Parkway
Cincinnati, OH 45226

RSVP
Junior League of Portland, Maine, Inc.
P.O. Box 677
Portland, ME 04104

SAVANNAH STYLE
Junior League of Savannah, Inc.
P.O. Box 1864, 41 W. Broad St.
Savannah, GA 31402

SEASONED WITH SUN
Junior League of El Paso, Inc.
520 Thunderbird
El Paso, TX 79912

SIMPLY SENSATIONAL
TWIGS, The Children's Medical Center
P.O. Box 750443
Dayton, OH 45475

ACKNOWLEDGMENTS

SOUTHERN ACCENT
Junior League of Pine Bluff, Inc.
P.O. Box 1693
Pine Bluff, AR 71613

SOUTHERN ELEGANCE
Junior League of Gaston County
P.O. Box 3684
Gastonia, NC 28053

TALK ABOUT GOOD
Junior League of Lafayette, Inc.
100 Felecie Dr.
Lafayette, LA 70506

TALK ABOUT GOOD II
Junior League of Lafayette, Inc.
100 Felecie Dr.
Lafayette, LA 70506

A TASTE OF NEW ENGLAND
Junior League of Worcester, Inc.
71 Pleasant St.
Worcester, MA 01609

A TOUCH OF ATLANTA
Marist School
3790 Ashford-Dunwoody Rd., N.E.
Atlanta, GA 30319-0047

VIRGINIA HOSPITALITY
Junior League of Hampton Roads, Inc.
1310-C Todds Lane
Hampton, VA 23666

VIRGINIA SEASONS
Junior League of Richmond
205 W. Franklin St.
Richmond, VA 23220

THE WILD WILD WEST
The Junior League of Odessa, Inc.
P.O. Box 13675
Odessa, TX 79768-3675

WOMAN'S EXCHANGE COOKBOOK, VOLUME II
Woman's Exchange of Memphis, Inc.
88 Racine St.
Memphis, TN 38111

INDEX

INDEX

INDEX

WIMMER BOOKS PLUS

ORDERED BY: (Please provide **complete street address** and print clearly)

Name ____________________

Address ____________________

City ____________________ State __________ Zip __________

Day Telephone ( ) ____________________

Title	Qty	Retail	Total	Title	Qty	Retail	Total
Soups	___	$5.95	_____	Chicken	___	$5.95	_____
Salads	___	$5.95	_____	Desserts	___	$5.95	_____
Vegetables	___	$5.95	_____	Meats	___	$5.95	_____
Breads	___	$5.95	_____	Seafood	___	$5.95	_____

Merchandise Total	$ __________
Shipping & Handling	$ __________
Sub-total	$ __________
TN residents add 8.25% tax	$ __________
TOTAL ENCLOSED	$ __________

SHIPPING & HANDLING

Order amount	Charge
up to $15.00	$3.60
15.01-25.00	4.20
25.01-40.00	4.80
40.01-55.00	5.60
55.01-80.00	6.40

THE KITCHEN COLLECTION

SEND TO: P.O. Box 18408 • Memphis, TN 38181-0408 • Phone: 901-362-8900 • Fax: 901-795-9806